Poems About Him

Krystal Nikol

Copyright © Krystal Nikol

ISBN- 978-0692164266

Photos by Necole Dash

Cover Design by Stephen Elugbemi

In Loving Memory of

Charles Edward Harris, Jr.

January 27, 1994 - May 3, 2015

"Just because someone desires you, it does not mean they value you."

- Nayyirah Waheed

"When we speak we are afraid our words will not be heard or welcomed. But when we are silent, we are still afraid. So it is better to speak, remembering we were never meant to survive."

- Audre Lorde

"I am about life. I'm gonna live as hard as I can and as full as I can until I die."

- Assata Shakur

Poems About Him

Table of Contents

A Happy Ending
Page Three

Lazarus
Page Four

Clarity
Page Five

Inheritance
Page Six

The World's Worst Apology
Page Nine

Twilight
Page Ten

Destiny
Page Eleven

Nomad
Page Twelve

Sea of Sorrow
Page Fifteen

Another Stupid Love Poem
Page Sixteen

Gold Diggin' in the Ghetto
Page Seventeen

Roses
Page Twenty

Blood
Page Twenty Three

Salvation
Page Twenty Five

Lust
Page Twenty Seven

Fluid
Page Twenty Eight

Erosion
Page Thirty

Whole
Page Thirty One

We
Page Thirty Two

Consent
Page Thirty Four

Betrayal
Page Thirty Five

Mo' Betta
Page Thirty Six

Abandoned, Building
Page Thirty Seven

Letter to My Youngest Brothers
Page Thirty Nine

Christmas
Page Forty

Affirmation
Page Forty Three

Matrimony
Page Forty Four

Reflection
Page Forty Seven

Juneteenth
Page Forty Nine

Poems About Him

My greatest fear is that

one day

they'll discover the poems I wrote

after I erased their capes

and identified their weaknesses

The poems

where they are no longer hero

become human

remain villain

remain inspiration

to fill post-its

and notebooks

and laptops

with enough stanzas

to write everything except

a happy ending.

Lazarus

Your wedding vows decay like bodies
in your family's mortuary
Your photo on the preacher's mantle
may as well be ashes
small remnants that are scattered
into Sunday dinner conversations
They hold memories
You hold on, loosely
You no longer keep your promises
You do not leave
but you do not love her anymore
(I hope.)

You tell everyone except the preacher's wife
You cannot disappoint your own mother
In an effort to keep them happy
you have embalmed yourself
used alcohol to hide your decomposition
Pretended that you are not dying
while expediting the process
The last time I drew your breath
I tasted whiskey, cigarettes and no regrets
watched the sunrise
and made no apologies
for attempting adultery
I smiled,
inhaled your scent in my sheets
and remembered what it felt like to be alive.

Clarity

From your tongue
my name
sounds like the best decision
my father ever made.

Inheritance

My grandfather
still places bets on his ex-wife
under the table
at the holiday photos he appears in
In a flash,
tells my grandmother
that they could be together

                                                  Again

She tells his third wife she would never
He will spend Christmas
with their family this year
I haven't opened presents
underneath his tree in a decade
But I won't tell him I miss him
He wouldn't do anything about it anyway
He'd rather call me brilliant behind my back
play telephone with compliments
instead of picking up
My father relays the message
says he's proud of me

                                                  Again

My uncle tells me I carry our name well
as if he knows it is a burden
tells me he loves me

calls me *mija*
reminds me that I am still his little girl
To him
I am still his little girl
whose diapers he changed
while she cried out for her daddy
Reminds me
that he was there when they were not
That's why it hurts more when we don't speak

My father
turns to his and admits
my mother was the only woman
he's ever truly loved
I pretend I'm not in earshot
that I have not settled for part time men
and called it romance
just to have a chance with someone like him
I've become expert at write-ins
made main characters of those
who visited my adolescence
made them superheroes
to justify their absence
as if I didn't need to be rescued
and raised

I watch my father
hold my little sister's hand
and pray she won't write this poem over
At least he's trying
My uncle still drinks

Krystal Nikol

says another shot cures the hangover
Their father still gambles
and might finally be running out of luck
They taught me
never to bet on black
men who wait for slurred tongues
to express how they feel
I'll only be disappointed
                                          Again.

The World's Worst Apology

I'm home waiting on you
That's why I told you to come here
with me

      Why are you up so early?

                    Hey baby
            I see I missed your call
                    I was just…

I'll be in your city this weekend

      What's up QUEEN?

        I don't know if that helps you
                        at all

What dat mouf do?

      I'm chillin'
Stop tellin' me to fuckin' chill

            I don't blame you

I'm at peace with it

      You made it home?

           Just thinking about you
           Miss you and all that

Twilight

I tiptoe on the
brink of insomnia and
insanity right

before sunrise so
I can meet you before I dream
and wait for your kiss

Goodnight

that never comes.

i

wonder

if

i

had

to

lose

you

to

become

me

destiny

Nomad

I saw Michelangelo carve ivory
then cover it in clouds
and place it behind your lips
At any time
you had the power
to light up a room
and permission
to leave me breathless

Your joy
beget happiness
beget memories
I've never felt more at home
than when your arms
wrapped around me
Made your embrace my address
Misunderstood "I miss you"
heard "I'll never leave you"
Misunderstood "I love you"
heard "I'll never leave you"
I took refuge in your body,
not knowing,

There is no place more dangerous for a
traveler to dwell.

You were the home
I always returned to
when I was sick of running
You are my first love.
You were...
Mine.

Then, somewhere in between
love letters
and prom pictures
and your 21st birthday
and California
and New York
and Texas
and finding myself,
I lost you.
I hugged your smile goodbye
Let it fall from my fingers one October
and I haven't seen it since

I saw her
in a picture
the day after my 23rd birthday
I've been writing this poem since
November 16, 2015
Hesitant to let my words
fall from the tip of this pen
because it hurts to train my tongue
to speak of you in past tense
to say you were...
I hope

she's everything your mother thought I wasn't.
I hope she loves you.
I hope she loves you out loud
not in the back
of an anxious poet's old tattered notebook
I hope she loves you onstage
with or without applause
without restraint

Today
was the first time your smile
brought me to tears
Your laugh
became an inside joke
I was not invited to
Your joy beget sadness
beget regret
beget pain

You parted your lips
and produced a hurricane
I am trying to survive
hoarding the pieces of me
that have not yet blown away
in your storm.

Sea of Sorrow

Nights were best
when we spent the hours
before closing our eyes
entangled in torn pages
disheveled sheets
critiquing lines
You let ink draw you out of depression
then shared with me in solace
and I bartered with everything
I'd finally found the courage to tell myself

We are still the closest thing to a love poem
I have ever written.

Another Stupid Love Poem

Fuck eleven. Fuck forbidden first dates. Fuck movie theaters. Fuck fifteen. Fuck first kisses. Fuck back seats. Fuck first kisses in backseats of first cars. Fuck fireworks. Fuck feelin' fireworks. Fuck July fourth. Fuck sweet sixteen. Fuck "I love you". Fuck missin' you. Fuck comin' back just for you. Fuck apologies and assorted bouquets. Fuck flowers. Fuck third base after third period. Fuck virginity. Fuck forehead kisses. Fuck prom. Fuck abstinence. Fuck waiting. Fuck June. Fuck an anniversary. Fuck graduation. Fuck celebrating. Fuck breakups. Fuck heartbreaks. Fuck holding on. Fuck holding hands. Fuck making up. Fuck eighteen. Fuck surprise parties. Fuck Valentine's Day. Fuck teddy bears. Fuck chocolates in heart shaped boxes. Fuck kissing when the ball drops. Fuck twenty-one. Fuck drunk texts. Fuck friends. Fuck this pen for writing another poem about you. Fuck everything that I once loved about you. Fuck love. Fuck forever. Fuck always. Fuck the photos that are still on my grandmother's mantle. Fuck tearstained pillow cases and sweat stained sheets. Fuck eleven years. Fuck friendship. Fuck three am. Fuck cuddling. Fuck calling you at three am to cuddle. Fuck missed calls. Fuck missing you. **FUCK YOU.**

Gold Diggin' in the Ghetto
(An Elegy for Jordan Davis)

People love gold diggin' in the ghetto.
Findin' treasures our grandparents built
then throwin' on a filter
Actin' like it's new
Tryna rename an' break ties
to make a mystery of the city's DNA
Labelin' it NoMa or SoHo
Callin' it Midtown.

Call me selfish,
I'll be Slum Village
Hoardin' hip hop,
The Sugar Hill Gang's ghetto baby,
forever.
'Cause I've seen
how country raise black children

Seen how mixed masters repeat beats
to break spines of songbooks
when they protest the notes
heard bullet break flesh when the beat bang
I still wanna know Jordan's favorite song
just don't wanna hear you sing it
or sample it
or profit from its people's problems
and use it as proof of progress
Oppression still hurts

even when I dance to it
even when it sound beautiful

Hip hop took its first
breath on these corners
now we can't afford to freestyle on 'em
Historic 'hoods changin' faces
gotchu thinkin' we goin' places
Took a bite from the Big Apple
Wanna see where Motown take ya?

I heard
the newspapers in Brooklyn
say Detroit is hiring

"Young professionals
passionate about the city's rebirth"

to direct Diaspora Displacement Disco
a Melanin Musical Chairs Emcee
to play Hipster Hip-Hop Hopscotch

This city ain't black and white Polaroids
It's people of color
not a blank slate to create
People of Detroit
have been murals for decades
Motown's top hits for centuries
When we bleedin' in the middle of the street
and you paint the town red
How you pretend your progress ain't killin' me?

How you kickin' people out their homes
and invitin' them to visit for a fee?

Then rappin' these lyrics loudly,
Puttin' on
like the instrumental don't inspire the hook
This is killin' the rose that grew from the
concrete
and tossin' me the bouquet
This is takin' from the ghetto,
pretendin' it has nothin' to give
Complainin' about the dirt
while minin' diamonds.

Roses

I ain't never liked flowers no way

                                        Petals collapse
                                        under the weight
                                   of pinky fingernails

This ain't no good gift

                                  How easily something
                                         beautiful can
                                      become broken

Just something else I must take care of
Another bud to feed
At this table
they become rotted

                                                Decayed
                                                 Fragile
                                                 Delicate

Centerpieces in my family dinners
remind me we don't gather often

Remind me of memorials
on the corner of
Canfield and Caddiefield
Teddy bears congregating
telling story by candle light
Reminds me that
bullets don't let black boys blossom
They tear thru flesh,
take both thorn and petal without regard
then leave sloppy arrangements
on cement blocks
for coroners to pick from
Ain't no bouquets 'round here
Just black on black protestors
at West Florissant
lookin' like family at a funeral procession

Look like my family
at my little cousin's funeral
gathered around his centerpiece of a body
Reminds me of mothers mourning
fathers hardened
My cousin speechless
as she watches the minister
lower her second son's casket
Ain't no gardens 'round here
just gravestones
Ain't no parks,
no playgrounds
just prisons by abandoned lots
and lots of liquor stores
on intersections without proper street signs

Krystal Nikol

we don't know which way to go
So we turn
on each other.

Roses ain't supposed to grow from concrete
so they pull triggers
to put orchids back in their place
My Auntie asked if I would
march for him like I marched for Mike
like cops and corner boys
ain't graduate from the same school of thought
taught that it's better to shoot first
and ask questions… maybe
They call us gangstas
Then arrive on scene
and cause crippling bloodshed

Black boys ain't allowed to bloom.
Black girls ain't free to grow here.
Black mothers plant their seeds then
produce the flowers used
to decorate the casket
Proves how easily something beautiful
can become broken
I ain't never like flowers no way
Reminds me of fragile.
Reminds me of delicate.
Reminds me of death.

Blood

He smiled

I returned a smile I did not feel

I didn't like

how his scent collided with mine

He was the first time I bled

Pain shooting

from his abdomen through my legs

Pressed

to a twin sized bed

by a man whose last name

I don't remember

Feigned sleep as he got dressed

to leave

the next morning

I lie still

as the night before

But this was the first time he noticed.

Krystal Nikol

I noticed

I have a nasty habit of euphemizing

when the truth sounds ugly

I'll tell my daughter

it was prom night

He kissed my forehead

before pictures

He kissed my lips in the limo

He kissed me gently

in our hotel room

Held my hand and reassured me

He took nothing

But gave an honest offering

and I did not bleed.

Salvation

*"Be not led astray
following temptation
when faith falters
don't allow despair to
divorce this holy union"*

Our children will worship
the God of our fathers.

Periodically
I am convinced
that a Black Jesus
thought enough of me
to barter his life
for my every breath
Temporarily
I find contentment in this
without searching further
But mostly
my mother's daughter
is who they pray for

We are the children
They prayed for
We leave choir stands in duets
before sermons start
to begin our own fellowship
and they pretend

Krystal Nikol

not to notice how
we hold hands past "Amen"
how we routinely appear just
before benediction

The deacon's youngest son
doesn't acknowledge my disbelief
and isn't deterred
from reading my palm with his pinky
when we hold hands
during consecration prayer
He still believes he is my communion
while I am unconvinced that
I'm in need of salvation

Lust

You hold secrets
on the roof of your mouth
that I can't wait
to taste
to trace
from biceps to fingertips
To hold on
to you
To be held in your arms
like it's two am again
      And I have no business being here
           And I don't intend to leave

Fluid

Preliminary shots
spill secrets before the first round
of jumbled, drunken memories
between muffled whispers
giggles
and open legs

        You held my hand during foreplay
                on the dance floor
    and I tried to beat you at your own game
          You caught me at each eight count
          Your hips told me you were better
                  Your grip told me
                      I could not escape
         Your lips told the back of my neck
            you knew I wouldn't even try
                  I'd found the artist
to finger paint the night's masterpiece

    I always become captivated by things
            that are out of my grasp

                  I've been here before
                    with someone else
        that was impossible to hold on to
                  Watching his chest rise

                    and fall rhythmically
while encased in his six-foot four-inch frame
          arms entangled in one another
              lower limbs outstretched
    while toes tamper with the foot board

At sunrise
I'll call you my favorite bad decision
then lick the taste of cognac
and you off my bottom lip
hoping you've forgotten everything
I spilled last night
or at least,
promise to keep my secrets.

Erosion

Water changes rock

It is altered. You and I

cannot stop flowing.

Whole

There are people
walking around with pieces of me
that I am in need of
but I cannot call
and ask of them
to return the fragments I gave
willingly.

My remnants
are slowly becoming a graveyard.

We

I. I smeared red lipstick on your collar
You kissed secrets behind my ear
as we stood in the kitchen
and waited for them to sing
and bring the cake
I took your necklace as a present
on my 21st birthday

II. We sat across from one another
at a college cafe
I laid my head on the wooden table
I knew I should not stay
But this sadistic love
we shared wouldn't let me leave
Shackled to you,
I felt captive
I didn't want to hear you admire her
I couldn't seem to escape

III. You said
that you haven't been in love
since her.
I became papier-mâché
under the weight of your words
barely able to hold it together
I cried until my eyes bled

wrote until my thoughts soaked the page
called out for you
and heard only my echo

IV. We woke up late
on a rainy Sunday morning
and Maroon 5 was playing on Pandora
You kissed my cheek and
I decided my to-do list was complete

V. I wasn't happy
I didn't know how to fix it
I was gone before I told you
I was leaving.

I did not say "No".
I was afraid you'd hear me
But would not listen.

Consent

Betrayal

I'm sorry

~~if you felt I hurt you~~

~~but what did you expect me to do~~

~~when you...~~

Mo' Betta

white people call the cops on Black people for doing what they've been doing in their neighborhoods before white people called cops on Black people doing what they've been doing in their neighborhoods before white people called cops on Black folks doing what they've been doing in their neighborhoods before white people called cops on Black folks for doin' what they've been doin' in their neighborhoods before white people called the cops on Black folks doin' what they've been doin' in their neighborhoods before white people called cops on Black folks doin' what they been doin' in they neighborhoods befo' white people called cops on Black folks doin' what they been doin' in they neighborhoods befo' white people called cops on Black folks doin' what they been doin' in they hood befo' wypipo called cops on Black folk doin' what they been doin' in they hood befo' wypipo

Abandoned, Building

His conversations deter me now
A compilation of indistinguishable moments
heard on my grandmother's police scanner
His arms are crossed caution tape
to deny access to anyone
who gets close enough to examine the scene

A boarded warehouse appears more
welcoming.

His embrace doesn't feel quite the same.
He doesn't smile like he used to.

So I want to hug him
until the sparkle returns to his eyes
and his cheeks no longer seem like a burden
to his unparted lips
Hug him
like the eight-year-old
with pigtails and dirty fingernails
and scuffed sneakers he just bought last month

I want to hug him back to my childhood
before he seemed shattered
by all that he's seen
in this city's
back alleys and broken bodies

Krystal Nikol

Before I became old enough
to understand
I am old enough for us to share a drink now
to leave the kid's table
and engage in stories
that were once deemed inappropriate
But he tells less jokes now
His conversations are warnings
and I'd rather laugh.

Letter to My Youngest Brothers
(A Poem for Xavier)

I cried
when I realized
I don't know you well enough
to finish a poem abou-

Krystal Nikol

Christmas
(Another Poem for Chuck)

In January
you turned 21
and older cousins are made
to celebrate that milestone
To be there
to light the trick candles
to enjoy the cake
to run interference when
the ugly chick at the bar
uses her eyelashes and a smile
to invite you to a dance
you never wanted
to buy your first legal drink
But you took this shot alone

On a neighborhood court
that prohibited liquor
he got drunk on testosterone
and defended his manhood
against your athleticism
During a layup
players are instructed to aim
for the upper corner of the box
Maybe coaches realize the detriment
when bullets hit directly in the center

To the boy who pulled the trigger
What was the point?
You took one of the greatest
players out of this game
And I will never forgive you
To the boy I missed turn to man
I am proud of you
I am so proud of you

I am angry
that my ears struggle to
remember the sound of your voice
My eyes recount fragmented
flashbacks of your smile
My back could not identify
your hands in a hug
Regret hangs from the tip of my tongue
like the last "I love you" never spoken
I want you to know how much I love you…
I want you to know how much I miss you.

Last time
we spoke was Christmas
and you told me next Christmas
you'd be home
To grab $20 and a toothbrush from Auntie Mimi
To fumble through grace without laughing
To fight over cherry cheesecake
and my mom's macaroni
and the next holiday movie

Krystal Nikol

The next time our family holds hands
around the dinner table
I pray for God
to send you from heaven
Let your wings
morph your body into precipitation
to stop the tears from falling
down your mother's cheeks
Take a seat,
grab her hand
you're the only present we need.

Affirmation

I've fallen in love before

Clumsily stumbled

into a man's embrace

and just stayed

This time,

I will go purposefully

Intentionally

into love with you.

Matrimony

I am barefoot
lace strewn between
freshly manicured toes
gold jewelry accents
a champagne colored,
mermaid style dress
with a cut-out
curls grace my shoulder blades
and hold the vale in place.

I carry a bouquet
of lilies and orchids,
sprinkled with white iris…
Because orchids are his favorite
I still hate flowers
but I carry a bouquet
because brides are supposed to
and it hides my sweaty palms

I proposed
to my bridesmaids at an open mic
said they were the icing
on this wedding cake
wrote a poem about how he loves me
like I love them
at one am emergencies
and five pm happy hours.
There are six of them

plus my maid of honor
who is reciting her toast to herself
She giggles as she realizes
that I can read her lips.
She winks.

Over my shoulder,
I steal glances at my brothers,
two on either side
of my mother's tear-filled eyes
I smile.
I can tell she is happy for me.
Eric Benet stops singing.

Who gives this woman away?

    Who gives this woman away?

        Who gives this woman away?

My heart explodes like beaches in Normandy.
Waves crash against the shore.
Birds croon overhead.
But the ceremony is quiet enough
to hear sand traverse an hour glass.
Time stops.

How do you give away something
that never belonged to you?
Bargain with property
you have rented on weekends?

Krystal Nikol

Give your name to a daughter
who dug you out of warnings
encoded in her mother's favorite gospel songs

Today,
I'll carry this bouquet
cause that's what brides are supposed to do.
But tradition won't walk this daughter
down the aisle
won't give away residual resentment.
I promised my husband
that I would allow him to love me
as if you never broke my heart.

I look up
His best man hands him a handkerchief
He wipes his eyes
and whispers that I'm beautiful
It is the sweetest charade
I have ever deciphered.

    Who gives this woman away?

    I say, "I do".

Reflection

I noticed
how my tone changes
when I speak about something
I am passionate about
I never heard that
when I spoke of you

                                                I have a tendency
                                                      to cut myself
                                          on shards of broken boys
                                     I try to hug into brilliant men

I still remember
the birthdays of old lovers
flames that flicker
threaten to reignite
annually

                                    I really wish I could hate you
                                      Hating you would be easier
                                           I can't wait to say
                                            "I don't love you"
                                                and mean it

I felt better today
but soon
I'll look for your touch
at the bottom of a bottle
trying to give us one last shot

It's two am
and you realize
everything you thought you knew
you don't
You'll be up for three more hours
looking for answers

Juneteenth

Rest in

Peace

Paradise

We change chants to fit her name

Protest the power structures

Police lines across the street

The audacity of the accused
to attempt to lead the funeral procession

The repast
is at the busiest intersection
downtown
to let the entire city
see what mourning looks like
when joy comes in it
Tears pool in our eyes
until we integrate our DNA
into the cement blocks
that we march on

You may not
have honored her alive
but tonight
You will feel her

Aura
In His name,
We pray
Amen.

A man
stands six feet over
smile taunting the traffic
He said her name
forced the city to
remember their transgressions

16 hours earlier
A nurse began a shift
at the hospital she just left
She cannot pass
She yells that she will be late for dinner
Sorry if this protest
delays her ride home,
it's not personal
But this is what it feels like to be immobile
illegitimate
unable to move freely

This is what it feels like
to be eaten alive
and we ain't burying black bodies
silently no more
So we scream
until crowds create chaos
and cuffs decorate his wrists

He is not read his rights
They will devise a justification
during their commute
They do not need one now.
This is what they do.

Black bodies decorate
precinct lawns like garden gnomes
waiting for an answer to come home
and kiss his daughter's forehead
Discuss tonight's decisions
Decide that if we could,
we'd go back in time
to see if our voices could
span the length of Michigan Avenue
See if vocal cords could suffocate
those who watch us suffer in silence
We sit solemn
unable to breathe until sunrise
on June 19th.

Acknowledgements
(*The Credits or*
The Back Sleeve of My Mixtape)

Foremost, I'd like to thank God; for the gifts, the courage and conviction to continue, especially when giving up felt like the easiest option.

To my family, who have been on my artistic journey since its inception; thank you! To my momma, the one, the only, Renae Antoinette; without you, I am nothing. Thank you to my Grandma (Shirley Bush), Grubby (Toni Davis), and Auntie (Kenna Micou) for being strong women who raise strong beautiful women. To my sister, Ja'Nae, you have been a protector, provider and a professional cheerleader throughout this post- graduate journey; thank you! For all the women who have loved and guided me, on purpose and by chance; thank you.

There's nothing like the family you choose for yourself! To Dailyn Danielle and Leyoun Dinzel, I love y'all immensely. Your friendships have meant more to me throughout these 16 (*gasps*) years than I can explain. Thank you for being.

To the squad- Pedro, Mitch, DeeRay, Chris, Jojo, Cherrelle and Leon...Thank y'all for listening to the many free writes and first drafts. Thanks for attending the open mics and the art shows. Kings and Queens, you are irreplaceable. You are appreciated. Royalty is LOYALTY!

To the poets! I won't be able to name you all, but I love you all. To G for founding The Poetry Society at EMU; thank you for planting the seed that grew into this. To Ami, for being the epitome of support. Thank you for believing in me when I didn't; the tough conversations, tougher love and motivation! To Jason "Squeeze" Ford, thank you for writing my favorite poem. To Nadine, your talent is beyond words, but what's better is your spirit. Thank you for the poem that introduced me to….Tiran, Brother Gabe, and Tiara. Thank y'all! For the years that we worked too hard and played too much, thank you. For "The Resurrection" which would not have been possible without Darius MUTHERFUCKIN Simpson. Thank you for the genuine, platonic love that pushed me through performances and protests. "First PS, then EMU, then The World!" and I mean that shit! Lil' Big Bro, I love you. To Jen and Shaina, thank you for reminding me that there is strength in being vulnerable, for being the support on both sides. To the future; Darion, Kenadi, Mercedes, Razjeá, thank you for letting me feel that this work was not in vain. For the many late nights and early mornings, rehearsals and recaps, performances and after parties, I am thankful to y'all. Grateful for y'all. I love y'all. WE ALWAYS WRITE!

To Necole Dash, thanks for the headshots and the opportunity to learn from an artist as talented and creative as you. To Steve Elugbemi, the man of many talents; thank you for the cover design, the poetry, and the group piece we still haven't finished. To AJ Ekokobe, thank you for the brilliant web design and the BEST TCOD that anyone has never seen.

To the many professionals who have contributed to my development and given me space to share my craft, thank you. Keith Jason, an advisor and friend, thank you. Dr. Melvin T. Peters, a genius, a teacher, a mentor, thank you! Thank you G, for accepting my work for "I'm Gorgeous; An Anthology Project". Thank you to Riverside Arts Gallery in Ypsilanti for The Black History Month Showcase. To Dr. Nicole April Carter for "My Mic Sounds Nice" and introducing me to the women of 5E Gallery in Detroit. To Phil Simpson and The Baltimore Gallery of Detroit for hosting "23: Art Exhibit and Poetry Slam". Elexus Anthony and "The Noire Thread" blog, Bee Roll, owner of Beezy's Cafe in Ypsi and all the artists that shared space at 23 North Washington Street; thank you! What we had was something special. May the growth we sustained and the art we created continue to carry us forward.

To every unofficial editor who has read a page, reviewed a section or named a poem, thank you for being part of this writing process. I appreciate your willingness to help "Poems About Him" to the final draft. Thank y'all.

Last but not least, thank you to everyone who inspired a piece, written or published, printed or performed. This would have been literally impossible without him.

-Krystal Nikol